At age seven, John Quincy Adams and his mother Abigail climbed Penn's Hill, just a short walk from their home. Together they watched in horror as Charlestown burned and smoke filled the sky during the Battle of Breeds Hill (Bunker Hill). John Quincy rode alone by horseback from Braintree (now Quincy) to Boston as a post-rider, hoping that a bundle of letters from his father awaited his arrival and he could return to his mother who waited anxiously at the farm for his return. From the time he was fourteen years old until his death at the age of eighty-one, John Quincy Adams, a child of the American Revolution, served his country. Arguably one of the most educated and experienced public figures in the United States, he continued the family tradition of civic responsibility and public service. Serving as minister abroad to the Netherlands, Prussia, Russia, and Great Britain, he negotiated treaties, including the Treaty of Ghent, which ended the War of 1812. As secretary of state, he defined America's foreign policy through his authorship of the Monroe Doctrine. His knowledge and understanding of the United States Constitution and diplomatic affairs contributed to his successful defense of the Mendi people who revolted aboard the slave ship *La Amistad* in 1839, in what became known as the *Amistad* Incident. The Boston Massacre case, argued by his father, and the Amistad Trial underscore both father's and son's belief in the right to representation. John Quincy continued his battle against the spread of slavery into his last days as a United States congressman, when he suffered a stroke and died two days later in the Speaker's Room of the United States Capitol.

This strong tradition of public service continued with John Quincy's son, Charles Francis Adams, who was appointed by President Abraham Lincoln as United States ambassador to Great Britain during the Civil War. He was the third generation of his family to serve in this post, which he held from 1861-1868. He successfully ensured England's neutrality and prevented England from providing financial support to the south, thus earning the title of "Great Ambassador."

Charles Francis Adams's sons Henry and Brooks Adams were both writers and historians. They provide a literary perspective on the Adams family and on nineteenth-century America through the turn of the century. Henry Adams is best known for his literary masterpiece, *History of the United States of America* (1801-1817), and his autobiographical work, *The Education of Henry Adams*, for which he received a Pulitzer Prize.

The story of the Adams family is compelling from a multitude of viewpoints, offering social, economic, literary, political, and personal perspective on the events and times that shaped our nation. Today, the historic homes, the Stone Library, a collection of personal belongings, and over thirteen acres of land are preserved, protected, and maintained under the stewardship of the National Park Service at Adams National Historical Park. The historic treasures that comprise this park offer visitors the opportunity to consider the achievement of each generation of this remarkable family, from the time they embarked on an epochal journey through their development into one of America's most prominent families.

John Adams

Abigail Adams

John Q. Adams

Charles Francis Adams

Henry Adams

Brooks Adams

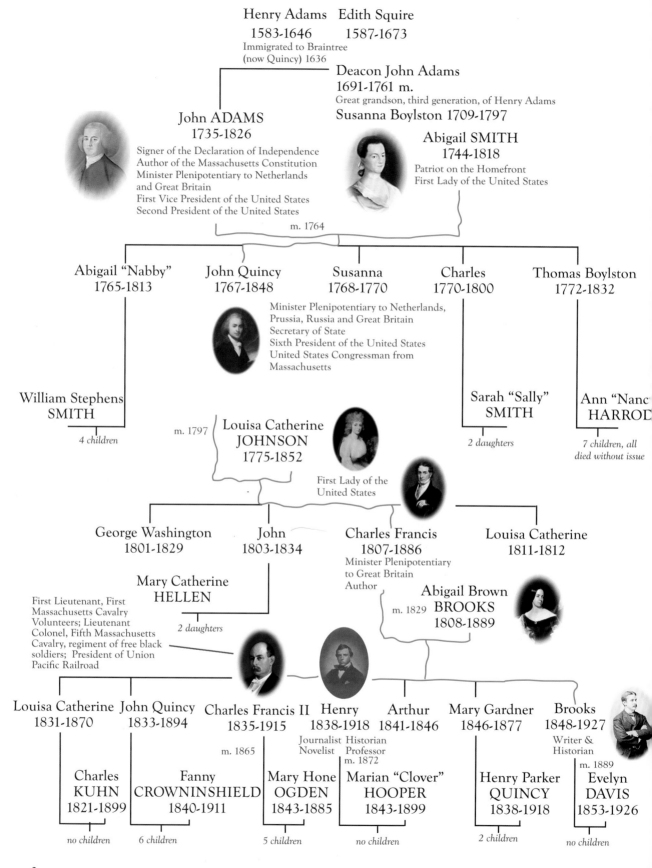

Henry Adams
1583-1646
Immigrated to Braintree
(now Quincy) 1636

Edith Squire
1587-1673

Deacon John Adams
1691-1761 m.
Great grandson, third generation, of Henry Adams
Susanna Boylston 1709-1797

John ADAMS
1735-1826
Signer of the Declaration of Independence
Author of the Massachusetts Constitution
Minister Plenipotentiary to Netherlands
and Great Britain
First Vice President of the United States
Second President of the United States

Abigail SMITH
1744-1818
Patriot on the Homefront
First Lady of the United States

m. 1764

Abigail "Nabby"
1765-1813

John Quincy
1767-1848
Minister Plenipotentiary to Netherlands,
Prussia, Russia and Great Britain
Secretary of State
Sixth President of the United States
United States Congressman from
Massachusetts

Susanna
1768-1770

Charles
1770-1800

Thomas Boylston
1772-1832

William Stephens
SMITH

4 children

m. 1797

Louisa Catherine
JOHNSON
1775-1852

First Lady of the
United States

Sarah "Sally"
SMITH

2 daughters

Ann "Nanc
HARROD

7 children, all
died without issue

George Washington
1801-1829

John
1803-1834

Charles Francis
1807-1886
Minister Plenipotentiary
to Great Britain
Author

Louisa Catherine
1811-1812

Mary Catherine
HELLEN

First Lieutenant, First
Massachusetts Cavalry
Volunteers; Lieutenant
Colonel, Fifth Massachusetts
Cavalry, regiment of free black
soldiers; President of Union
Pacific Railroad

2 daughters

m. 1829

Abigail Brown
BROOKS
1808-1889

Louisa Catherine
1831-1870

John Quincy
1833-1894

Charles Francis II
1835-1915

Henry
1838-1918
Journalist
Novelist

Arthur
1841-1846

Mary Gardner
1846-1877

Brooks
1848-1927
Writer &
Historian

Historian
Professor
m. 1872

m. 1865

m. 1889

Charles
KUHN
1821-1899

Fanny
CROWNINSHIELD
1840-1911

Mary Hone
OGDEN
1843-1885

Marian "Clover"
HOOPER
1843-1899

Henry Parker
QUINCY
1838-1918

Evelyn
DAVIS
1853-1926

no children

6 children

5 children

no children

2 children

no children

Early Quincy, Massachusetts

Quincy, MA. *From Nature* by E. Whitefield.

Boston

The Old House at Peace field. *View In Oils* by G.N. Frankenstein, 1849.

John Adams Birthplace (right) and John Quincy Adams Birthplace (left).
Oil painting by G.N. Frankenstein, 1849.

What is today Quincy, Massachusetts (formally Braintree), was first inhabited by the Massachusetts tribe of the Algonquin Indians. The earliest English settlers arrived on its shores in 1625. The Old Coast Road was the only road connecting the rural community to Boston, ten miles north, and the settlement of Plymouth, thirty miles south. Travel to Boston was two hours by foot, and less by horseback. The outside world had little impact on this remote community, and in turn the community had little impact on the outside world. Three hundred and fifty years later, three unassuming homes sit quietly beside the road: the John Adams and John Quincy Adams Birthplaces and the Old House at Peace field. The occupants of these homes have long since passed, but their story is preserved within the architecture, the cultural landscape, and the extensive museum collection, all of which serve as the backdrop to the story of colonial America and the birth of a nation.

John Adams and John Quincy Adams Birthplaces

John Adams (right) and John Quincy Adams (left) Birthplaces. Watercolor by Eliza Quincy, 1822.

The boyhood homes of two United States presidents, the father and son John and John Quincy Adams, can be seen today on Franklin Street, set back only a few feet from the Old Coast Road. These two seventeenth-century houses are in the saltbox style, so named because of the sloping gabled roof that gives the house the shape of a wooden box used to store salt during colonial times. A common home style, particularly in New England, the slope results from a one-story addition to the rear of the building. Only seventy-five yards separate the John Adams Birthplace from the John Quincy Adams Birthplace. It is within these two simple, unassuming cottages at the foot of Penn's Hill that two young boys, both future presidents, learned the core values that would serve as their moral compasses as they navigated through life's challenges.

During the Revolutionary War, the location of these homes on the main road from Boston to Plymouth placed Abigail Adams on the front line of action. It is here that Abigail, both astute in her observations and intelligent in her writing, shared with husband John and ultimately the Continental Congress the progress of the war on the homefront. "You give me more public intelligence than anybody," John Adams wrote to Abigail on September 7, 1783.

Today, these two cottages are the oldest presidential birthplaces in the United States. They sit in their original locations. Little is left of the one hundred forty acres of farm and woodland that supported the family for over eighty years. The furnishings are simple and sparse. The richness of these homes is communicated through the written record of the occupants. While living in these cottages, John, Abigail, and their son John Quincy Adams wrote extensively about their lives and experiences. In more than twelve hundred surviving letters, numerous diaries, and memoirs they furnish the homes and paint the landscape with literary eloquence. Often separated from each other by great distances, they used their writings to communicate individual experiences and matters of the heart. One cannot overestimate the importance of these writings to the survival of their family, nor can one overlook the importance of these letters to future generations and the study of history.

John Adams Birthplace

The house was built ca. 1681. In 1740, Deacon John Adams, great grandson to Henry Adams (1583-1646), purchased this home with six acres of farmland. There, he and his wife, Susanna Boylston, raised their three children, John Adams, future second president of the United States, Peter Boylston, and Elihu.

Typical of the time, Deacon John Adams farmed in the summer and worked at his trade as a cordwainer (shoemaker) in the winter. During his lifetime, he increased the size of his farm from 6 to 188 acres of arable fields, orchard, salt marsh, meadow, and woodland. The diverse landscape provided for the family's basic needs of food, water, wood for cooking and heating the home, fertilizer, and feed for farm animals. To a young child, the land was a playground for adventure and discovery. Describing his youth, John Adams writes that it "went off like a fairy tale" and of feeling the joy in "making and flying Kites, in driving hoops, playing marbles, playing Quoits, Wrestling, Swimming, Skating."

Deacon John Adams did not venture far from his home but was active in the community. He held positions in two of the most important institutions in town, serving as selectman and deacon at the parish church, located less than a mile from his home. His involvement in community affairs made a strong impression on John Adams, who wrote, "my father who had a publick Soul had drawn my attention to Public affairs, from my earliest Infancy, took the Newspapers and gave them to me to read – so that I became some what attentive to publick affairs."

Younger brothers Peter Boylston and Elihu were expected to be farmers like their father, while family tradition determined that John Adams, as eldest son, would be provided with an education. At six years old, he attended Dame Belcher's school just across the street from his home and learned to read, write, and work on arithmetic. He transferred to Braintree's Latin School, conducted by Joseph Cleverly, whom Adams described as negligent and cross. Soon John began to lose his interest in books. He asked his father if he could study under Mr. Joseph Marsh, who ran a private boarding school only two doors down and across the road from his home. The next morning, Deacon John informed his son that the arrangements had been made and he was to report to school that morning. John Adams thrived under the tutelage of his new schoolmaster and was, at the age of fifteen years, deemed ready for Harvard.

Having just been defeated for a second term as United States president in 1801, John Adams reflected on his father's trade: "If I were to go over my Life again I would be a Shoemaker rather than an American Statesman."

Walnut cradle, made by a village coffin maker. According to family tradition, it was used to rock four generations of the Adams family, including both presidents.

John Adams was academically shaped by his formal schooling, but in character, morality, and service to community no one had a greater influence on John Adams than his father, whom he described as "the honestest Man I ever knew," and his mother, who no doubt influenced his belief that "Mothers are the earliest and most important Instructors of youth." His mother's "Countenance and Conversation was a Source of Enjoyment."

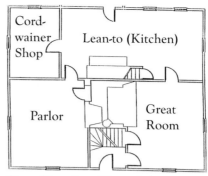

Floor Plan, First Floor. John Adams was born October 30, 1735, in the southeast bedchamber located directly above the Great Room.

The John Adams Birthplace is a typical seventeenth-century house, two rooms wide by one room deep, with a hall and parlor and a partial lean-to addition. The lean-to provided much needed space for Deacon John Adams when ecclesiastical councils were held at his home. His will lists twenty-three chairs, unusual for such a humble household but necessary to accommodate the members of the councils. As an adolescent, John Adams was witness to these meetings, one of which played a decisive role in his choice of a career. Reverend Lemuel Briant served as a minister to the church of Quincy. Liberal in his theology and embracing the spirit of the Great Awakening, he alienated many of his parishioners, eventually leading to his resignation. As John Adams considered

Lean-to interior extending along the back of the house.

a career in the ministry, which his father expected, he recalled the Briant controversy: "Very strong doubts arose in my mind, whether I was made for a Pulpit in such times, and I began to think of other Professions. I perceived very clearly, as I thought, that the study of Theology and the pursuit of it as a Profession would involve me in endless Altercations and make my Life miserable, without any prospect of doing any good to my fellow Men." John Adams would choose a profession he determined more suitable to his temperament.

Having earned his A.B. degree from Harvard College in 1755 at the age of twenty years, John Adams assumed the job of Latin master for the grammar school in Worcester, MA, a sixty mile, one-day journey by horseback from Braintree. While holding this position, John Adams signed on to study law under attorney James Putnam

for a fee of one hundred dollars, and in two years time his studies were complete. Returning home to Braintree and settling in with his mother and father, John Adams was admitted to the bar on November 6, 1759, and had his first case within weeks.

Soon after his return home, John Adams was awakened from his sleep to the "severe shock of an Earthquake. It continued nearly four minutes.... The house seemed to rock and reel and crack as if it would fall to ruins about us." John Adams' words were prophetic. Soon, the political and emotional ties between the mother country and her colonies would "rock, and reel and crack," and from the ruins would emerge a nation. John Adams and his family would come to embody the strength of character and determination residing in the founding fathers and mothers.

John Quincy Adams Birthplace

John Quincy Adams Birthplace, built in 1663. Law office door is on the left side of house.

Abigail Adams. Pastel by Benjamin Blyth, 1766. Courtesy of the Massachusetts Historical Society.

John Adams. Pastel by Benjamin Blyth, 1766. Courtesy of the Massachusetts Historical Society.

Deacon John Adams purchased the Belcher house next to his homestead in 1744. On May 25, 1761, John Adams' father passed away at the age of seventy. John Adams inherited this cottage, only seventy-five yards from his own birthplace, with forty acres of land – ten adjoining the cottage plus thirty of orchard, pasture, woodland, and swamp. It is here he brought his bride, Abigail Smith Adams, upon their marriage on October 25, 1764. A daughter Abigail, whom they nicknamed "Nabby," was born within the first year. John Quincy, future sixth president of the United States, followed. A little girl, Susannah, "called Suky," died just after her first birthday. Charles and Thomas completed their family of four.

John Adams established a thriving law practice in his home. His office book for 1770-1774 shows sixty cases in July and seventy-eight in September 1772. While Abigail tended to their children, John was occupied with clients in the next room, rendering the four-room cottage busy with children and clients. John Adams installed a door in his law office so his clients could come and go without disturbing the rest of the family. Except for duties during the first ten years of their marriage that sometimes required him to travel to the Superior Court in Boston or ride circuit from Maine to New Jersey, John remained close to home. Although accustomed to short periods of separation, nothing could have prepared John and Abigail for what was ahead. Soon their lives were interrupted by events that would transform their scene of domestic tranquility into the turbulent landscape of the Revolutionary War.

John Adams' law office with his stand-up law desk, where he wrote the Massachusetts Constitution in 1779.

Silver tankard which belonged to Abigail Adams' father and mother. Made by John Noyes, Boston, 1700-1710. It is one of three examples of Noyes' workmanship in existence today.

Two lists of law actions belonging to John Adams for February 1772 and February 1773.

Burdened with heavy debt resulting from the French and Indian War, Great Britain sought opportunities to reduce this tremendous debt, and King George III imposed a series of taxes on the colonies. Tensions escalated, and the Boston Massacre of March 5, 1770, erased any lingering doubt that this struggle would require bloodshed. Amidst the chaos of accusation and propaganda surrounding the Massacre, John Adams emerged on the scene as an independent thinker who would not be led by the majority, but instead, by the law. Successfully defending the troops accused of the Boston Massacre, John Adams was recognized as one of the leading attorneys in Massachusetts. In the fall of 1772, the people of Massachusetts elected John Adams to represent them at the First and Second Continental Congresses in Philadelphia, Pennsylvania, where Adams would next earn the reputation as the "Coleuses of Independence."

John and Abigail Adams would spend the second ten years of their marriage with "The great distance between us," as Abigail wrote in August 1774. Separated first by three hundred miles (Philadelphia) and later three thousand miles (Europe), John Adams played a pivotal role in American independence, subsequent peace negotiations between England and the new United States of America, and the establishment of American diplomacy. During this time, Abigail maintained their farm, educated their children and cared for family members and community.

Kitchen, John Quincy Adams Birthplace.

I find myself weary of this wandering Life.
My heart is at Home.
John Adams to Abigail, July 1771

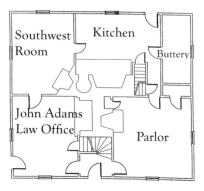

Floor plan, first floor. John Quincy Adams was born July 11, 1767, in the northeast bedroom located directly above the parlor.

Locket given to Abigail Adams by John Adams on his departure for Europe to serve as peace commissioner. The painting is done with hair. The reverse reads: "Hair of John and Abigail Adams."

Parlor, John Quincy Adams Birthplace.

John Quincy Adams. Pastel by Isaak Schmidt, 1783.

John Quincy Adams' baptismal gown, on loan from Independence National Historical Park.

Bullet mold used by Abigail Adams to make bullets for use in the American Revolution.

Early on in the Revolution, John Adams wrote a plea to Abigail: "I must intreat you my dear Partner, in all the Joys and Sorrows, Prosperity and Adversity of my Life, to take a Part with me in the Struggle." Eventually, Abigail Adams took part in the struggle in ways that neither of them could have imagined.

During the ten year absence of her husband, Abigail Adams assumed many roles as "Patriot on the Home front." She had a unique vantage point from her "little cottage" at the foot of Penn's Hill. Abigail was brilliant in her ability to manage the household, the farm, and the education of her children. As "farmeress," she oversaw one hundred and eight acres of farmland, at a time when farmhands were scarce. With schools closed, Abigail began the early education of her four small children in her parlor. As "School Mistress," she taught her children reading, writing, mathematics, Latin, and French. Progressive in her views on education, she wrote to John of her desire "that our new Constitution may be distinguished for learning and virtue. If we mean to have Heroes, Statesman and Philosophers, we should have learned women." Her library included Shakespeare's *The Tempest, Much Ado About Nothing,* and *King Lear*; Milton's *Paradise Lost*; and Thomas Paine's *Common Sense.*

Abigail and John shared an unusual relationship, where opinions were freely expressed and each influenced the other. On the eve of American independence from Great Britain, Abigail wrote to John, "And by the way in the new Code of Laws which I suppose it will be necessary for you to make I desire you would Remember the Ladies." It was not a demand for political or social equality; it was a plea for humane treatment.

In addition to caring for her family and the farm, Abigail provided food and shelter to the colonial militia and refugees fleeing from Boston.

She described her life on the homefront as a "scene of confusion." Her letters to John from March 3-5, 1776, provide a vivid picture of her reality:

"I have just returnd from Penn's Hill where I have been sitting to hear the amazing roar of cannon and from whence I could see every shell which was been thrown...How many of our dear country men must fall...I went to bed about 12 and rose again a little after one. I could no more sleep than if I had been in the ingagement. The ratling of the windows, the jar of the house and the continual roar of 24 pounders, the Bursting of shells give us such Ideas, and realize a scene to us of which we could scarcly form any conception. About Six this morning, there was quiet; I rejoiced in a few hours calm."

Abigail and John Adams experienced the Revolutionary War in dramatically different ways, as revealed in their correspondence. They each provide a lens of perspective in communicating the uncertainty and fragility of the "Glorious Cause" for which they sacrificed so much.

Eleven years after John Adams left his wife and family to join the fight for independence, he successfully negotiated the Paris Peace Treaty, ending the Revolutionary War. He quickly summoned Abigail to join him in England, writing "Will you come to me in the fall...with my dear Abby?"

Abigail and daughter Abby (Nabby) departed for Europe to be joined with John Adams after a separation of ten years. Upon seeing her husband and son, Jonn Quincy, Abigail described the reunion in a letter to her sister Mary Cranch: "Poets and painters wisely draw a veil over those scenes which surpass the pen of one or the pecil of the other; we are indeed a very happy family once more."

The Old House at Peace field

*I think to christen my Place by the name of Peace
field, in commemoration of the Peace which I as-
sisted in making in 1783, of the thirteen Years Peace
and Neutrality which I have contributed to preserve,
and of the constant Peace and Tranquility which I
have enjoyed in this Residence.*
John Adams Diary, September 8, 1796.

Subsequent to their return from Europe
to the United States in 1788, Abigail and John
Adams successfully negotiated the purchase of
a new residence, just 1 1/2 miles north of the
"little cottage" that was their home for the first
twenty years of their marriage. Beginning with
John and Abigail, four generations of the Adams
family found a place of private refuge from the
arena of their public lives at Peace field. Called
the Old House by later generations, the home
and grounds at Peace field embody the Adams
spirit of public service, their connection to each
other, and the legacy each generation strived to
honor. Before his death in 1927, Brooks Adams,
great-great grandson of John Adams, established
the Adams Memorial Society whose charge was to
care for the Old House, grounds, garden, orchard,
Stone Library, and personal possessions belonging to the Adams family. Recognizing the national significance of the Adams story, the Memorial
Society, consisting of members of the Adams family, donated Peace field including the Old House,

Stone Library, contents, and 4.77 acres of the
original estate, to the people of the United States
in 1946 under the stewardship of the National
Park Service.

Prior to John and Abigail Adams'
purchase in 1787, the Vassall-Borland
Estate was recognized as one of the finest
country homes in rural Braintree (which
became Quincy in 1792). Built in 1731 as
a summer residence by Leonard Vassall, a
sugar plantation owner from the West Indies
who immigrated to Boston, the home was
inherited by his daughter Anna Vassall. After
she married John Borland in February 1749,
they took up residence in her family home.
When John Borland received a substantial
inheritance at his father's death, he and Anna
moved to Cambridge, Massachusetts, in 1765.
During the next ten years, they presumably
leased the house to tenant farmers. The
Vassall Borlands were Loyalists to the King
of England during the Revolutionary War;
with the death of her husband in 1775 and
mounting hostility from the patriots, Anna
fled to England, where she remained for seven
years. As was common during this time, the
Vassall-Borland estate was confiscated, both
to prevent destruction as well as to provide
housing for refugees fleeing from the British
in Boston. James Bowdoin, chairman of the
committee that drafted the Massachusetts
Constitution and second governor of
Massachusetts, stayed at the house for two
weeks during the Revolutionary War in 1775.

When the war came to an end, Anna
Borland returned to Boston to reclaim her
estate and then gave it to her son, Leonard
Vassall Borland. Abigail and John Adams
purchased the home in 1787. Their grandson
Charles Francis Adams later built a new
house nearby, and thereafter family members
began referring to the house at Peace field as
the Old House.

The Old House at Peace field.
Braintree by E. Malcom, 1798.

The Old House at Peace field was built in 1731 as a summer residence by Leonard Vassall. Just ten miles south of Boston, the country home was recognized as one of the finest in rural Braintree (which became Quincy in 1792). Abigail and John were especially attracted to the seventy-five acres of farm land, including "a great variety of fruit trees" and farm buildings which would support this working farm.

The home was a three-story frame building with brick chimneys on the east and west ends. Seven rooms made up the home of 1731: two rooms on the first floor, two on the second, and three smaller rooms in the third floor garret. A detached kitchen was located behind the main house on the north side (customary in warmer climates). It was attached to the main house sometime within the first thirty five years after the home was built. Each generation of the Adams family left an imprint on the home, reflecting the lifestyle of the period. Although the structure was enlarged from the original seven rooms to the present twenty-one rooms, remarkably the additions were executed in such a way as to compliment the original footprint of the home. The hallways connecting each addition made to the Old House provide a seamless transition, underscoring the family's sensitivity to maintaining the integrity of their ancestral home.

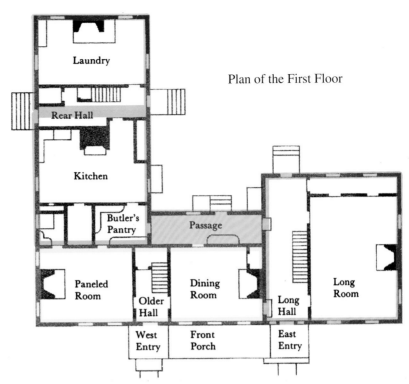

Plan of the First Floor

Additions made to the Old House

1731-1787 The Vassall-Borland period original home
Kitchen Wing 1737-1765
1800 East Wing Addition, John and Abigail Adams
1836 Hallway Addition, John Quincy Adams
1869 Servants Wing Addition, Charles Francis Adams

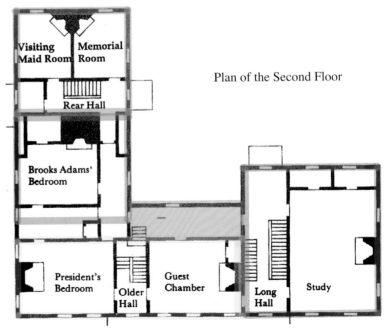

Plan of the Second Floor

Paneled Room

When the 1731 front door to the Old House opens, one is immediately immersed in the world of the Adamses. The home serves as a backdrop to the Adams family saga, blending eighteenth-, ninteenth-, and early twentith-century life and providing meaning and context for their story.

To the left of the front door, the floor-to-ceiling San Domingo mahogany wood paneling draws the eye to the Paneled Room. When John and Abigail Adams first arrived in September of 1788, this was one of two rooms on the first floor serving as a keeping parlor and dining room. Unlike the next three generations, they would live in the home year-round. To bring more light into the room, especially during the long, cold, New England winters, John and Abigail added a window on each side of the fireplace. The

dark wood paneling was whitewashed and later restored by grandson Charles Francis Adams. Abigail could be found shelling her beans in this room, "without ceremony or apology," in preparation for dinner parties for family and dignitaries alike. They dined with President James Monroe, Commodore Perry, General Sumner, John Coles (Secretary to President Madison), and his brother, Edward Coles. It was at this gathering with the Cole brothers in the summer of 1811 that John Adams said of Thomas Jefferson, "I have always loved Jefferson, and I still love him," extending the olive branch to Jefferson after ten years of estrangement. When Revolutionary War hero General Marquis de Lafayette dined with John Adams on August 29, 1824, the two comrades reflected on the old days of the revolution.

American camel back sofa in Chippendale style, 1765-1785. It was here John Adams sat for Gilbert Stuart to paint his portrait in 1823.

Portrait of John Adams in his eighty-eigth year by Jane Stuart after original by Gilbert Stuart.

Seventy years after his father John Adams successfully defended the British troops accused of the Boston Massacre, John Quincy Adams welcomed Ellis Loring and Lewis Tappan of the *Amistad* Committee to his home in November 1841. They would ultimately convince John Quincy that his knowledge of the United States Constitution and law, as well as his diplomatic skill, was critical to the successful defense of the Mendi people in the United States Supreme Court Case of the *Amistad*. Just six years later, John Quincy would celebrate his eightieth birthday in the Paneled Room, rising and toasting his guests: "Ladies and Gentlemen, I thank you all for your good wishes, which I reciprocate by hoping you will all live to be eighty years of age, and then be surrounded by friends as near and dear to you, as those I see around me."

Henry Adams, in his *The Education of Henry Adams*, published in 1907 and named best book of the twentieth century by the Intercollegiate Studies Institute, wrote of his grandmother, Louisa Catherine Adams, wife of John Quincy, "Sitting in the Panelled Room, at breakfast, with her heavy silver teapot and sugar-bowl and cream jug... To the boy she seemed singularly peaceful, a vision of silver gray, presiding over her old President and her Queene Anne Mahogany."

Brooks Adams, the last generation of the Adams family to live in the Old House, resisted the rapid pace of commerce and industry and the impact it was having on the rural community of Quincy. Describing this age of progress as "creeping destruction," he worked to preserve the historic integrity of his ancestors' home and treated the Paneled Room as a time capsule, never allowing the use of gas or electric lighting. Instead, he favored the warm glow of candle flame reflecting off the mahogany paneling.

The eighteenth-century atmosphere preserved in this room provides the perfect setting to consider moments in history that are both intimate and revealing and have an importance and relevance that transcend time.

English tea set brought from England by Louisa Catherine Adams.

Dining Room

Abigail Adams' mahogany dining table in the center of the room surrounded by her son John Quincy Adams' Sheraton Empire chairs was the setting for numerous family gatherings, reunions, and celebrations. One can imagine the conversations that took place at this table, surrounded by portraits of four United States presidents: George Washington, John Adams, John Quincy Adams, and James Monroe. The portraits of John Adams and Washington draw attention upon entering the room. The placement of these portraits on opposite ends of the room facing each other is symbolic of the historic moment in history when the United States witnessed the first peaceful transfer of power between one executive and another with the inauguration of second United States President John Adams in 1799.

Sterling silver pitcher and tray, 1879. A gift from the children of Mr. and Mrs. Charles Francis Adams specially made to celebrate their parents' golden wedding anniversary.

Eighteenth-century Chippendale mirror belonging to Abigail Adams.

President George Washington, oil painting by Edward Savage, 1790. Commissioned by Vice President John Adams. Price tag on back of painting. John Adams paid 46 2/3 dollars for this painting and an accompanying one of Martha Washington.

Candlabra, English cut glass, 1765-1785.

Mahogany dining room table, 1785-1810, belonged to John and Abigail Adams and was used by successive generations.

The Gilbert Stuart portrait of John Adams at age eighty-eight hangs in a place of honor above the fireplace. Viewing the portrait of himself, John Adams reflected on his life in public service and its impact on his family when he wrote, "It seems to me at this time to have been awlfully wicked to have left such a wife and such a family as I did, but, I did so in the service of my country." This was the last portrait painted of John Adams, as he died just three years later at the age of ninety-one.

Pair of American knife cases belonging to John Quincy Adams. They were used in the White House by John Adams.

Pitcher belonging to Mr. and Mrs. Charles Francis Adams, 1828-1832. An example of early American fine porcelain, produced in the United States by William Ellis Tucker of Philadelphia.

Eighteenth-century Chinese serving dishes belonging to John and Abigail Adams.

Northeast view of Dining Room with Abigail Adams' mahogany table. Wrought-iron gas chandelier added in 1860 by Charles Francis Adams. Above the fireplace is the last portrait of John Adams, at the age of eighty-eight. This oil painting is a copy of an original painted by Gilbert Stuart at the request of John Quincy Adams; Stuart's daughter Jane created the copy.

Long Room

Having lived in two spacious homes while abroad in France and England, Abigail was "sadly disappointed" with the limited space of her new home at Peace field, writing her daughter Nabby, that "in height and breadth, it feels like a wren's house." The addition of the East Wing in 1800 provided Abigail and John Adams with a formal parlor (Long Room) on the first floor, a study on the second floor, and additional bed chambers on the third floor. Measuring approximately thirty-two feet long by thirty-two feet wide and elegantly furnished, the Long Room was designed as a public room for entertaining. When Revolutionary War hero General Marquis de Lafayette made his final tour of the United States in 1824, John Adams hosted a reception for him at Peace field. Grandson Charles Francis Adams, then seventeen years old, recorded in his diary the sight of these distinguished men sharing dinner at the dining room table and afterwards the Marquis, standing in front of the Long Room fireplace, "saluting the ladies" of Quincy.

Southeast view of the Long Room. A four-seated ottoman upholstered in green velvet was brought back from England by Mrs. Charles Francis Adams in 1868. Holding a place of honor above the fireplace is a portrait of Dr. Joseph Warren, who was friend and physician to the Adams family and a general who died while fighting at the Battle of Breeds (Bunkers) Hill, June 17, 1775.

When 240 West Point cadets marched from New York to Boston in 1821, they detoured to Peace field to pay their respects to former Commander-in-Chief John Adams. At eighty-five years old, Adams addressed the cadets on the south portico, congratulating them on "the great advantages you possess for attaining eminence in letters and science, as well as in arms. These advantages are a precious deposit, which you ought to consider as a sacred trust, for which you are responsible to your country and to a higher tribunal." Daughter-in-law Louisa Catherine Adams left an account of the visit, recording the menu: "Hams, Tongues, Beef Cheese, (small) Bread, Crackers, Coffee, Chocolate, Limondae, Punch, and Winte."

President James Monroe and poet Ralph Waldo Emerson each paid visits to John Adams to congratulate him on the election of his son John Quincy Adams as sixth President of the United States.

Eighteenth-century pole fire screens belonging to Abigail Adams.

Abigail Adams Smith (Nabby), daughter of John and Abigail Adams, oil painting by Mather Brown, 1785.

Nathaniel Gorham, attributed to Charles Wilson Peale ca. 1787. Gorham was grandfather to Abigail Brooks Adams, served in the Continental Congress (1782 and 1785-87), and was elected president of Congress in 1787, serving seven years.

Great grandmother of Abigail Adams. Mary Mason, artist unknown, 1668.

The family portraits that adorn the walls of the Long Room are a reminder that the Old House was a family home to four generations of the Adams family. The Long Room was a place where family traditions were celebrated. The first of several family weddings was the marriage of Caroline Smith, Abigail and John Adams' granddaughter and daughter of "Nabby," to William Smith. Four golden wedding anniversaries were celebrated in this room, and the family danced together in celebration of John Quincy Adams' eighty-eightith birthday. The Long Room was also the setting for solemn gatherings. Surrounded by images of their beloved family members, generations of Adamses found comfort as they gathered together for private farewells to Nabby in 1813, Abigail in 1818, John in 1826, and John Quincy in 1848.

One of twelve Louie IV chairs, 1764-1778, purchased by John Adams for the Hague Embassy in 1783-1784.

West view of Long Room. Oil paintings from left to right: *Abigail Adams* by Jane Stuart, 1800-1812; *John Quincy Adams*, copy of John Singleton Copley, ca. 1796; *John Adams* by Jane Stuart, ca. 1800; *Charles Francis Adams* by Charles Bird King, 1827. Below the John Quincy portrait is a Louis XV settee, 1764-1778, purchased by John Adams when serving as minister plenipotentiary to the Netherlands at the Hague.

Long Hall

Abigail Brooks Adams, oil on canvas by William Morris Hunt, 1872.

Between the busts of John Adams and George Washington is the 1826 memorial wreath made by the students of the Seminary for Female Education in Bethlehem, Pennsylvania. The wreath was presented to First Lady Louisa Catherine Adams upon the death of her father-in-law John Adams in 1826. While serving as a member of the Second Continental Congress, John Adams visited the school in 1777.

Plaster bust of John Adams by Binon. On May 29, 1818, John Adams wrote Thomas Jefferson, "Mr. Binon, a French Artist, from Lyons who has studied Eight years in Italy has lately taken My Bust. He appears to be an Artist and a Man of Letters. I let them do what they please with my old head."

Charles Francis Adams, oil on canvas by Frederick P. Vinton, 1879.

Louisa Catherine (Johnson) Adams, oil on canvas in gilt and black frame by Edward Savage, ca. 1794.

The Long Hall connects Abigail Adams' 1800 addition (Long Room and Study) to the original 1731 home. The Dutch table, 1775-1790 is attributed to John Adams.

Study

Serving as the "summer White House" for both Presidents John Adams and John Quincy Adams, the study provided an atmosphere conducive to the daily work demands of the office of the presidency. The study was also the intellectual setting where four generations of Adams pursued their literary interests, surrounded by their books.

Defeated for a second term as United States president, John Adams would consider his future when he wrote, "The only question remaining with me is what shall I do with myself?" John Adams returned to Peace field. Retired from public life and busy with family and farm for the next twenty-five years, he never lost his interest in government. Seated at his writing desk in the northeast corner of the study, Adams put his pen to paper and stayed connected to his contemporaries, even renewing old friendships. One such friendship was with Thomas Jefferson. The two elder statesman engaged in a correspondence that produced a total of 329 letters in ten years. Their letters are an elegant testament to a friendship born on the eve of the American Revolution and enduring for more

than fifty years. Adams and Jefferson each offer a distinct perspective on the political landscape of the new republic, still in its infancy and fertile ground for debate and political rhetoric. Both Adams and Jefferson peel away the rhetoric and provide context and meaning to the events of the Revolutionary War and birth of a nation.

In one of the more poignant moments in American history, these two patriots died on the same day, July 4th 1826, on the fiftieth anniversary of the adoption of the Declaration of Independence. Years earlier John Adams instructed his son John Quincy on the value of books when he wrote, "You will never be alone with a poet in your pocket." John Adams did not die alone. At approximately 6:20 in the evening, he died peacefully, surrounded by his family and his books.

Northeast view of Study. Henry Adams' desk is in the center of the room. The barrel-back mahogany chair was used by John Quincy Adams.

Secretary (Escritoire), 1775. John Adams' desk purchased in France about 1784. It has always been in the northeast corner of the Study and it was here that John Adams carried on his correspondence with Thomas Jefferson from 1812-1826.

Southeast View of Study

Southeast view of Study with Henry Adams' desk in center and John Adams' highboy, 1735-1765, beside the front window. It was family custom never to polish brass, both for fear of harming the wood and giving the appearance of affluence.

John Quincy Adams' terrestrial globe contains the latest discoveries and communications from the observations and surveys to the year 1799, by Captain Cook...and navigators engraved from a drawing by Mr. Arrowsmith, geographer, to 1807. A Celestial Globe (not pictured) contains the positions of nearly 6,000 stars.

Framed lock of John Adams' hair, cut on July 5, 1826, the day after he died.

John Adams's wing chair, 1780-1790, where just a few days before his death, he gave his last message to the American people: "I give you Independence forever."

President's Bedroom

The southern exposure of the two front windows of the President's Bedroom welcome the brilliant sunlight for much of the day, creating a tranquil atmosphere rich in color and texture. The windows on either side of the fireplace, on the west wall, were added by John and Abigail Adams. The late afternoon sun is softened to a warm glow, casting orange and yellow hues throughout the room as the sun disappears on the horizon.

Southwest view of the President's Bedroom. Dutch bed, 1775-1785, purchased by John Adams as Minister Plenipotentiary to the Netherlands. Upon this bed Abigail Adams died on October 28, 1818, and Abigail Brooks Adams on June 1, 1889.

Abigail and John Adams shared their last days together in this room, before Abigail succumbed to typhoid fever on October 28, 1818, at the age of seventy four. Just three days earlier, Abigail and John celebrated fifty four years of marriage. Adams' despair at the loss of the "dear Partner of my Life" is palpable in the words he wrote to Jefferson, "I believe in God and in his wisdom and benevolence and I cannot conceive that such a Being could make such a species as the human merely to live and die on this earth." Adams hoped he would meet Abigail again in a "future State."

Warming pan, 1765, a wedding gift to Abigail Adams. Inscription in center ring: Abigail Adams, 23, October, 1764.

Around the fireplace are the tiles bought by John Quincy Adams in Liverpool, 1801, for his mother, Abigail. The Iron back bearing the date 1788 commemorates the date John and Abigail Adams moved into the Old House.

Scene from Silesia, with view of Falkenberge Mountains, steel engraving, by Berger after original water color painting by Reinhardt, 1798. One of four purchases by John Quincy Adams while in Prussia (today part of Germany and Poland) serving as United States Minister.

Henry Adams Bedroom

Henry Brooks Adams (1838-1918), photographer unknown.

Henry Adams concluded in his Pulitzer Prize-winning work, *The Education of Henry Adams,* that his formal education, which emphasized the classics, history, and literature, left him unprepared for the scientific and technological breakthroughs of the late nineteenth and early twentieth centuries. As an adult, Henry Adams embarked on a life-long journey of self-directed education, traveling the globe and seeking understanding and solutions through first-hand experience. As a history professor at Harvard, Henry introduced his students to an innovative teaching method of discussion and understanding instead of lecture and memorization. At the death of his father Charles Francis Adams in 1886, Henry was summoned home by brother Brooks to help care for their ailing mother, who would survive her husband by only three years. It was during this time that Henry penned his nine volume *History of the United States,* in the Stone Library. Upon completion of this work, Henry wrote in his journal, "I walked among the yellow and red autumn flowers, blazing in sunshine, and meditated," referring to the nineteenth-century English garden, designed by his mother and just beyond the doorstep of the Stone Library.

Heart-shaped tea cup, one of a set of five used by Henry and Clover Adams, Clarence King, and John and Clara Hay, as members of the "Five of Hearts."

French Ormolu clock, Empire design with porcelain dial, given to Henry Adams by his grandfather, John Quincy Adams.

Bronze medallion caricature by Augustus Saint-Gaudens, 1904. The angel wings on the porcupine body capture the contrasts of Adams's personality.

View of north wall of Henry Adams Bedroom located on the third floor. A complete set of *The North American Review,* from 1816-1877, is in the left bookcase. Henry Adams served as editor from 1870-1876.

Brooks Adams Bedroom

Western view of bedroom. The Empire-style four post bed (1815-1830) and English traveling case (1785-1810) on the left side of the window belonged to John Quincy Adams.

Brooks Adams, writer, historian, lecturer at Boston University School of Law, and adviser to President Theodore Roosevelt, was the last of four generations of the Adams family to reside at the Old House. The youngest of seven children, he assumed responsibility of his ancestral home upon the death of his parents, Charles Francis and Abigail Brooks Adams. During the forty-one years of his stewardship, he made yearly excursions abroad to Europe and the Far East, where he studied architecture. Photographs of Chartres, Rheims, and Peterboro adorn the walls and reflect his interest in European cathedrals. Reflecting to his brother Henry, he wrote: "On the whole, the parts of my life which I look back to with the greatest delight are those I have spent among the churches and castles of the Middle Ages."

Brooks preferred this bedroom because it provided the best view of his mother's nineteenth-century English garden, which Brooks called his "outdoor livingroom."

View of formal garden from Brooks' bedroom window.

Print of the official White House portrait of President Theodore Roosevelt by John Singer Sargent, presented to Mrs. Brooks Adams in 1903.

Kitchen

As technology progressed through the eighteenth, nineteenth, and early twentieth centuries, modern conveniences eased life for the wealthy and many home kitchens were transformed, leaving little evidence of the past. This was not the fate of the Kitchen in the Old House. Instead, the Kitchen is preserved as a time line for domestic technology spanning three centuries. Abigail Adams' 1780 reflector oven stands beside the Model 50 Walker and Pratt stove, added between 1848 to 1850 and the gas stove added in 1915. The 1852 gas lines for the lighting still remain, although electricity was introduced to the house in 1915.

West view of Kitchen. Tall clock, ca. 1680, signed William Mason/London.

Left to right: Gas stove, Walker and Pratt stove, and reflector oven.

The servants bell system was added in 1850 by Charles Francis Adams, at a cost of $23.50. Behind each bell are the initials of each room. Each bell sounds a different ring for each room, and the little wooden ball continues to swing after the bell is silent, allowing extra time for slower servants.

1869 Servants' Wing

Each generation of the Adamses who occupied the Old House made additions to the original seven-room home. Third generation Charles Francis and Abigail Brooks Adams made the last addition, a three-story servants' wing, adding maids' living quarters, a visiting maid's bedroom, a servant's bathroom, and a laundry room, for a total of twenty-one rooms in the home today. Many of the Adams household servants were of Irish descent, reflecting the wave of immigration to Boston following the 1845 Potato Famine.

West view of laundry room showing Walker and Pratt Model 50 stove with six flatirons, ca. 1850, and portion of Empire sofa used for guests of household servants, ca. 1840. Forth generation Brooks and Evelyn Adams employed a laundress whose only responsibility was to do the laundry work and prepare dinner on Thursday evening when the cook was out. Nora Schofield served in this position from 1920-1927. At the end of every day, she packed up the laundry and cleared the room to be used as a sitting room for the maids.

Sewing Room and visiting Maid's Bedroom. Above the mantlepiece is an engraving titled *Eruption du Mont Etna de 1766*, engraved by J.B. Chapuy from a painting by A. D'Anna.

Originally the Head Lady's Maid Room, the Memorial Room, is home to family objects that reflect four generations of public service. The portrait above the fireplace is of Mary Ogden Abbott, by Alfred Collins. She was the last Adams to be born in the Old House. The swords on the mantlepiece were given to Charles Francis Adams Jr. by his brother John Quincy when Charles joined the First Massachusetts Cavalry in 1862.

Guest Bedroom

The furnishings in the Guest Room recall the diplomatic service of the Adams family. Although called a "guest room," it was primarily used by family members visiting and living at the Old House. During the eight years following the death of Abigail, John Adams welcomed back sixteen of their children and grandchildren who slept among the treasures of this room at different times.

Toilet set, with bleeding heart decoration, mid-nineteenth century. Brought from England by Mrs. Charles Francis Adams, 1868. Charles Francis Adams served as United States Ambassador to England, 1861-1868.

Mahogany sleigh bed, received by Peter Chardon Brooks as partial payment of a debt owed to him by Daniel Webster. The knitted bedspread is the work of Louisa Catherine Adams.

Dutch Louis IV style chairs, 1760-1775, are a reminder of John Adams' mission as first United States minister plenipotentiary to the Netherlands at the Hague.

Reflections of Travel

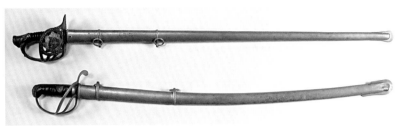

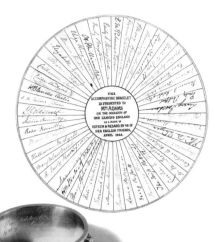

Swords given to Charles Francis Adams Junior by brother John Quincy Adams II when he joined the First Massachusetts Cavalry in 1862.

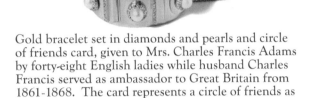

Gold bracelet set in diamonds and pearls and circle of friends card, given to Mrs. Charles Francis Adams by forty-eight English ladies while husband Charles Francis served as ambassador to Great Britain from 1861-1868. The card represents a circle of friends as well as equality of friendship.

Traveler's case used by John Adams with initials IA, possible Latin use of I for J, ca. 1785.

American Flag that Charles Francis Adams took to England during the Civil War. He served as United States ambassador to England from 1861-1868.

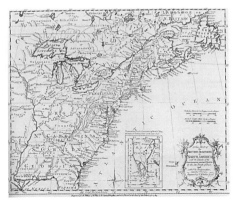

English traveling case, 1785-1810. Used by John Quincy Adams during his European travels. Includes many compartments and parts such as wash basin, writing surface, inkwell, and dressing glass.

Russian passport authorizing Louisa Catherine Adams and her eight-year-old son, Charles Francis, to proceed from St. Petersburg to Paris in 1815 to meet John Quincy Adams, who was negotiating the Treaty of Ghent, which ended the War of 1812.

Mitchell Treaty map, 1775. Used by John Adams as minister plenipotentiary to Great Britain during peace negotiations in 1782.

Passages

The hallways of the Old House provide a physical link between the original building and new sections added by each generation of the Adams family.

1836 Hallway added by John Quincy Adams to allow passage between the President's Bedroom and the Study without interrupting guests in the Guest Room. The hallway is lined with bookshelves holding the library of Brooks Adams, who enjoyed reading late into the evenings and wanted his books close at hand. The old pine hutch belonged to Abigail Adams.

1731 Entry to the Old House. Family lore holds that only members of the Adams family use this historic staircase in order to preserve the carpet. Carpet added by Mrs. Charles Francis Adams, June 1861.

1731 second floor landing with Benjamin Willard Clock, 1770-1785.

1836 Butler's Pantry connecting the Kitchen to the Dining Room.

1870 Stone Library

During summer and fall, the Stone Library is draped in a fragrant veil of wisteria vine, subtlety complementing its architectural beauty. Measuring thirty-eight feet long and twenty-five feet deep, it maintains a powerful presence in the landscape. Extending upward from the wisteria vines is an imposing slated gable roof, supported by granite corbel below the trim and brick gable ends with granite coping. Extending from the library into the garden is the granite entry, simultaneously mysterious and inviting, suggesting something magnificent to explore.

The 12,000 books, pamphlets, manuscripts, and maps in the Stone Library were collected and read by four generations of Adams men, women, and children. These books were read in pursuit of knowledge and understanding as well as for pleasure and enjoyment and reflect the literary tastes and genius of the family. Subjects include history, biography, classics, poetry, theatre, geography, travel, fiction, philosophy, religion, science, diplomatic and United States documents, works of American statesmen, and family writings.

Photo by Nancy Sentry.

North view of Stone Library: Built by Charles Francis Adams at the request of his father, John Quincy Adams, it is the intellectual reservoir for four generations of the Adams family. Designed by Boston architect Edward C. Cabot it is made of Quincy granite and brick masonry with a slate roof.

1870 Stone Library Interior

To enter the Stone Library is to step into the literary world of the Adams family. Visitors are treated to an array of pleasing sensations. The eye will marvel at the colorful spectacle created by the books, portraits, geometric tile floor design, and warm golden hue of the floor-to-ceiling oak shelving reflecting the sunlight entering from three French windows and a skylight.

The aroma of the sixteenth- to twentieth-century leather bindings and oils from the oak shelving and library table permeate the atmosphere and evoke an extraordinary awareness of the Adams' fundamental belief in the power of education to transform the world.

Presiding over the library, above the center table, is a portrait of President John Adams, painted by William Winstanley in Philadelphia in 1798. Below are two busts of John Quincy Adams, the one on the right created by Cardelli in 1818 and the one on the left produced by Hiram Powers in 1873. The oak library table was custom made for the library and used by Charles Francis Adams as he edited the papers of his father and grandfather, which were entitled *Works*

John Quincy Adams, bust by Hiram Powers, 1873. Revealing the strain of his unyielding fight for the repeal of the Gag Rule (1835-1844), which prevented any discussion of slavery in Congress, John Quincy dedicated a poem to the artist in 1837: "Sculptor, thy hand has moulded into form the haggard features of a toil-worn face, And whosoever views thy work shall trace an age of Sorrow, and a life of Storm."

of John Adams (ten volumes) and *Memoirs of John Quincy Adams* (twelve volumes). Continuing the family tradition of literary accomplishments, Henry Adams completed the final pages of his critically acclaimed nine-volume *History of the United States* in the Stone Library.

The "Mendi Bible" was a gift to John Quincy Adams from the Mendi people of Africa. Kidnapped from their homeland to be sold as slaves, they subsequently revolted aboard the slave ship *La Amistad*. John Quincy Adams successfully defended the Mendi captives in the United States Supreme Court in Washington, DC, in 1841.

American Commissioners at the Preliminary Peace Negotiations with Great Britain, by Benjamin West, 1783. Copy made for J. P. Morgan. From left to right are John Jay, John Adams, Bejamin Franklin, Henry Laurens, and William Temple Franklin. The English delegation is not shown as both Richard Oswald and Caleb Whitefoord died before West could make a sketch of them.

There were no official seals for missions. As peace commissioner, John Adams used the Boylston family seal of his mother, Susanna Boylston, to sign the Treaty of Paris, 1783.

Copy of *Cortege funebre de feu sa majeste l,empereur Alexandre I er de glorieuse memoirs,* including hand-colored plates of each section of the funeral procession of Alexander I in 1826. It was presented to President John Quincy Adams by the Russian government.

Bronze statuary. The Adamses were well versed in the writings of the great philosophers, orators, and poets, the hallmark of the traditional classical education they enjoyed. There are more than ninety volumes and over one hundred shelves devoted to the classics. The "household gods," as John Quincy referred to his bronze statuary of Cicero, Homer, Plato, Virgil, Socrates, and Demosthenes, are displayed on the fireplace mantle and underscore their influence on the political thought of both John Quincy Adams and his father, John Adams, as seen throughout their public careers and in their writing. The nineteenth-century French bronze sculpture in the center of the mantle belonged to Henry Adams and represents a remarkable collection of decorative art collected by the Adams family.

Desks – A Family of Writers

John Adams

"Dissertation on the Canon and the Feudal Law," 1765
"Novangtus" essays, 1775
"Thoughts on Government," 1776
"Massachusetts Constitution," 1780
"Letters from a Distinguished American," 1782
A Defence of the Constitutions of the United States,
3 volumes, 1787
Discourses on Davila, 1791

John Quincy Adams

"Publicola" essays
"Marcellus" essays
"Lectures on Rhetoric and Oratory," 1806-1809
Report on Weights and Measures, 1821
The Duplicate Letters, the Fisheries and the
Mississippi, 1822
"The Wants of Man," poem 1841
Letters of John Quincy Adams, To His Son
on The Bible and Its Teachings, 1850
Poems of Religion and Society, 1853

Louisa Catherine Adams
Narrative of a Journey from Russia to France, 1815
The Adventures of a Nobody, 1809-1812
Poems

Charles Francis Adams

Letters of Mrs. Adams, 1840
The Works of John Adams, 10 volumes, 1850-1856
Memoirs of John Quincy Adams, 12 volumes, 1874-1877

Henry B Adams

Democracy: An American Novel, 1880
"Captain John Smith," 1867
The Life of Albert Gallatin, 1879
Esther: A Novel, 1884
History of the United States, 1889
Mont Saint Michel and Chartres, 1904
Education of Henry Adams, 1907
"A Letter to American Teachers of History," 1910

Brooks Adams

The Emancipation of Massachusetts, 1887
Law of Civilization and Decay, 1895
The Degradation of the Democratic Dogma, 1920 *America's*
Economic Supremacy, 1900
The New Empire, 1902
Theory of Social Revolutions, 1913

Secretary used by John Adams for correspondence with friends and contemporaries including Thomas Jefferson, Mercy Otis Warren, and family.

Louisa Catherine Adams' Massachusetts-made mahogany secretary, 1795-1810. Henry Adams, in his *Education* describes his grandmother sitting at the desk: "She stayed much in her own room with the Dutch tiles*, looking out on her garden with the box walks."

John Adams, eighteenth-century stand-up law desk, used when he was a young lawyer, later as President of the United States, to hold state papers; and where he drafted the Massachusettts Constitution in 1779.

Early nineteenth-century French library desk belonging to Henry Adams and sent to the Old House from his Paris apartment.

Brooks Adams purchased this Chippendale-style desk for his mother, Abigail Brooks Adams; it is located in the Paneled Room with a view of the garden.

*English tiles made by James Sadler of Liverpool

Peace field: From Working Farm to Country Estate to National Park

John and Abigail Adams, 1787-1826

Oh, my sweet little farm, what I would not give to enjoy thee without interruption?

U.S. Vice President John Adams, Philadelphia, PA to Abigail, Quincy, MA, February 27, 1793.

The Adams Seat in Quincy, Massachusetts, by Mrs. G.W. Whitney, 1828.

Although John Adams' life in public service often required long absences from his farm in Quincy, his heart and spirit remained deeply connected to the soil of his youth. As a young boy, he found the rewards of satisfaction and fulfillment from working the land. When asked by his father what he would be when he grew up, John Adams answered with great pride, "a Farmer." The next morning, father and son spent a hard and very muddy day harvesting Creek Thatch. When his father asked him if he was still satisfied to be a farmer, young John replied, "I like it very well Sir." His father replied, "Aye but I don't like is so well: so you shall go to School to day."

Many years later, at the age of fifty-three, John Adams and wife Abigail returned from England following ten years of public service at home and abroad. They took up residence in their new home, which included seventy-five acres of farmland, meadow, woodlands, marsh, orchard, and garden. Within the year, John Adams was elected first vice president of the United States and, eight years later, the second president. He wrote to Abigail from Philadelphia, PA, in 1794, "I begin now to think all the time lost that is not employed in Farming. Innocent, healthy, gay elegant Amusement! Enchanting Employment! How my Imagination roves over my rocky mountains and through by brushy meadows." These next twelve years would be spent traveling back and forth from the farm at Peace field to New York, Philadelphia, and Washington, DC, in the service of his country as vice president and president.

Abigail Adams 1801 Abigail Adams brought a clipping from a York rose bush and planted it in her garden upon her return from England in 1788.

As time allowed, usually in the summer months and later during a retirement of some twenty-five years, John and Abigail ran their farm. To the west of the house, English boxwood shrubs, planted in 1731, form four rectangular beds, which were filled with fruit trees including apple, pear, plum, and peach and with cowslip, daffodils, and columbine flowers throughout. Abigail wrote of the property "containing the best collection of fruit in town." Each fall, cider was milled from the apples, and in 1799 Abigail made certain that eight or nine of the fifty barrels of cider were stored in the cellar for John, who adopted the practice of a morning Jill of cider to dissolve any phlegm in his stomach. He noted in his diary that it caused "no ill but some good Effect."

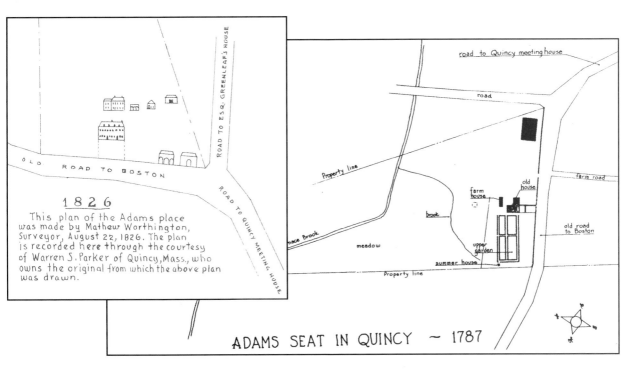

1826

This plan of the Adams place was made by Mathew Worthington, Surveyor, August 22, 1826. The plan is recorded here through the courtesy of Warren S. Parker of Quincy, Mass., who owns the original from which the above plan was drawn.

ADAMS SEAT IN QUINCY ～ 1787

Among the orchard and boxwoods to the west of the Old House, Abigail kept a kitchen garden, which provided fresh herbs and vegetables for their table. Returning home to Peace field following her husband's defeat to serve a second term as United States president, she reported to son-in-law Colonel William Smith," I have commenced my operations of dairy-woman; and she [Nabby] might see me, at five o'clock in the morning, skimming my milk." She supervised the making of butter, cheese, and jam.

John Adams worked alongside the farmhands and in 1796 transformed the large meadow north of the home into a cornfield. After five days of ploughing with the help of seven to ten yoke of oxen, the meadow was ready for planting. Some thirty years before as a young boy, John Adams viewed the work of a farmer as honorable. Although his destiny led him to Harvard University, Philadelphia, Europe, and Washington, DC, he longed to return to the place of his youth. Finally, the elder statesman could be found riding his horse Cleopatra through the fields and meadows and the Blue Hills to the north where, he wrote: "no Place has any Charms for me ... My Heart will have forever, an acking Void, in any other place."

View of orchard with drying yard and clothesline attributed to Abigail Adams.

1799 Woodshed, the only outbuilding remaining from John Adams' farm.

John Quincy and Louisa Catherine Adams, 1826-1848

I want a garden and a park
My dwelling to surround ~
A thousand acres (bless the mark!)
With walls encompassed round,
Where flocks may range and herds may low,
And kids and lambkins play ~
And flowers and fruits commingled grow,
All Eden to display.

John Quincy Adams, *The Wants of Man*

Drawing by Sarah Apthrop, 1837, showing farm buildings and grassy area in the barnyard where John Quincy Adams planted his "Seminary."

Formal garden with yellowood tree (right) which Louisa Catherine Adams brought back to the Old House from Washington, DC and the black walnut tree (left) planted by John Quincy Adams.

Unlike his mother and father, John Quincy Adams did not live at the Peace field year round. His interests lay not in the vegetable garden and farming but instead in trees. Visiting only during summer months, John Quincy and his wife Louisa Catherine did not need to harvest the trees for firewood, but instead valued their aesthetic quality and importance in national defense. During this period in American history, military strength was determined by sea power, and ships were made of wood.

John Quincy Adams observed the barren landscape surrounding his home where stately trees once formed the backdrop to Peace field. Thereafter, he set out to "plant trees for future generations," a motto adopted from Tacitus. He established a nursery on an old "summer house" foundation at the west end of the garden and planted a variety of seedlings including althea, apple, ash, beech, chestnut, cherry, elm, locust, maple, oak, peach, pear, plum, walnut, horse chestnut, and buttonwood. The seedlings were taken from this nursery and planted in his "Seminary" on the eastern side of the house, between the farm buildings. The seminary was "laid out in 8 rows each of 8 rings... Each ring ...about 4 feet in diameter, dug three feet deep, and filled with manure and fresh earth mixed up with the old soil."

John Quincy Adams did not take much interest in flowers because "they pass off and perish

leaving nothing behind..." Trees, however, "one hundred years hence will bear deliciust fruit, or afford a shelter and shade [to] ages of men." Like the tree, John Quincy Adams's contributions to his country are permanent and continue to be meaningful and relevant to "ages of men."

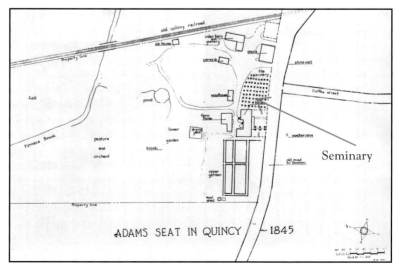

Seminary

ADAMS SEAT IN QUINCY / ~ 1845

Charles Francis and Abigail Brooks Adams, 1848-1889

1849 daguerreotype of the Old House, by Mr. Whipple.

> *One thing that is particularly noticeable with me of late years, and that is how greatly my local attachments to scenery have increased around me. I never enjoyed sky, and air and scene, in other words mere luxury of living, as I have the past two years.*
>
> Diary of Charles Francis Adams, November 1858, Quincy, MA

During the residence of Charles Francis and Abigail Brooks Adams, from 1848-1889, Peace field underwent a dramatic transformation from a working farm to a gentleman's country estate. The marriage of Charles Francis Adams to Abigail Brown Brooks brought great wealth to the Adams family and provided the means to finance changes to the property that would accommodate their affluent lifestyle. A Servants' Wing with six bedrooms and a laundry room was added to the Old House in 1869, serving a staff of at least five maids who accompanied the Adamses on their annual summer excursions from Boston to Quincy. The orchard extended up the northern slope behind the Old House and into the garden. When the Stone Library was constructed in 1870, some of the fruit trees from the orchard were moved from this area to the north of the new library. This section of the orchard and vegetable garden was replaced with the present day nineteenth-century style English garden.

Impressed with the English country estates they saw when Charles Francis Adams served as United States minister to England (1861-1868), Mr. and Mrs. Adams were unhappy with the clutter of the farm buildings on the east side of the home. Distant cousin and renowned landscape architect Andrew Jackson Downing visited the Old House, and suggested a landscape design for a "park like setting." Farm buildings were razed and replaced with a manicured lawn and a "park of trees," including horse chestnut, elms, and oaks. The construction of the 1873 Carriage House completed the transformation

of Peace field, with only John Adams' 1799 woodshed remaining as a reminder of the working farm.

1873 Carriage House

Charles Francis Adams recorded in his financial diary in 1868 the purchase of a carriage at a cost of $1,000, although he had no place to keep it. He engaged the firm Cummings and Sears to design the combination Victorian English Gothic and Norman style Carriage House, which was built in 1873, the last of the outbuildings to be added to Peace field. This brick, fieldstone, and granite U-shaped building measures ninety-five feet by fifty-five feet, providing space for horses, cows and goats on the north section (left), a carriage room (center), and coachman's quarters on the south (right). The ground floor provided space for cows and goats, and as late as 1920, milk for the table came from cows.

Coachman to Brooks Adams, perhaps waiting to "drive out" Brooks Adams to the Blue Hills. Like great-grandfather John Adams, Brooks was very fond of the Blue Hills.

North section of Carriage House with four open stalls for work horses and two large square stalls for the carriage horses. Brooks Adams reserved a large stall for his favorite horse, a bay mare named Beauty, so she would have room to move around. Such was his love of Beauty that he left an inheritance of $20,000 for her care and benefit.

Brooks and Evelyn Adams, 1889-1927

I have seen many places, but of its kind, representing what it does, the first century of the republic, the home of three generations of New England gentlemen, I know nothing to equal it here or elsewhere. It is complete, unique, and charming.

Brooks Adams to brother Henry, April 15, 1906

Late nineteenth- and early twentieth-century Quincy experienced a change in industry and land-use practices that would influence the once rural landscape of the community. World War I saw the shipbuilding industry surpass the once thriving granite industry, and the need to house the thousands of employees caused a construction boom. Residential homes replaced the old farms that once defined the area. The town of Quincy officially became the city of Quincy in 1888.

In response to the changing landscape, and revealing his own struggle to make sense of the rapid pace of American life, Brooks showed great restraint in regard to change and viewed Peace field as a time capsule of a vanishing lifestyle and the Adams family legacy of public service. He embraced the "peace and tranquility" of the home and garden and worked to keep what he described as "creeping destruction" from penetrating into the comforting world of his ancestral home. Brooks replaced the open-latticed fence in front of the Old House with a tall brick wall and large wooden gates topped with urns, which provided privacy and protection from the busy street.

In the early 1920s, the construction of Furnace Brook Parkway to the north of Peace field redirected the old brook that once passed through the middle of the property just north of the Old House. This cut off 6.94 acres of the estate, which was eventually sold off and developed. Today, Furnace Brook forms the northern boundary of Adams National Historical Park.

Concerned about what would happen to the Old House when he was gone, Brooks consulted with a variety of people whose suggestions included donating the dutch chest to a museum and removing the mahogany paneling and giving it to another museum. Brooks replied: "The chest and mahogany paneling would be too unhappy if taken from their home of so many years." He finally concluded, "I will not fret longer about the Old House, the library and garden; my family has always met its responsibilities."

To ensure the continued protection and future care of the Old House at Peace field, Brooks established what would become the Adams Memorial Society, whose mission was to open the Old House and Stone Library as an "educational and civic center." The Adams Memorial Society, still active today, was formed on March 28, 1927. Recognizing the national and international significance of the home, the Adams Memorial Society donated the Old House and its contents, the grounds, and Stone Library to the National Park Service in 1946.